How To Raise A Happy Genius Core Life Skills Training

A Self-Control Development Programme For Primary Classrooms

Dr Colin M. Drysdale

Pictish Beast Publications

Text Copyright © 2019 Colin M. Drysdale
Imprint and Layout Copyright © 2019 Colin M. Drysdale/Pictish Beast Publications

All rights reserved.

This book has been specifically produced for use in primary school classrooms. This means that the cost of this book includes the right to photocopy its contents to produce handouts for use in classrooms and for other educational purposes. However, they cannot be reproduced for any 'for-profit' activity without express permission.

ISBN – 978-1-909832-69-5

Published by Pictish Beast Publications, Glasgow, UK.
Published in the United Kingdom

First Printing: 2019. First Edition.

The cover image is copyright © C.M.Drysdale/*www.HowToRaiseAHappyGenius.com*

www.PictishBeastPublications.com

Table of Contents

        Page

1. What you will find in this book — 1

2. What is self-control and why is it important for children to learn this life skill? — 2

3. How does this programme help develop good self-control skills? — 4

4. What to tell parents/carers about the importance of self-control development and the contents of this programme — 7

5. The self-control development programme — 13

6. How to encourage your students to invent their own self-control development games — 43

7. How to help your students track their self-control skills development — 44

8. Integrating self-control development into the rest of your teaching — 48

9. Additional reading on self-control and its importance for child development — 59

---- Chapter One ----
What You Will Find In This Book

This book provides all the information you need to introduce a self-control development programme into your primary classroom. The optimal age for doing this will vary from child to child, but it is typically when children are in primary two, three or four. However, this programme can be done with children as young as primary one and as old as primary six. The first section (chapters two to four) provides background information for this self-control development programme. In it, you will find information about what self-control is and why it is such an important life skill for your students to develop. Information is also provided on how you can explain the importance of self-control development to parents and carers. This includes a four-page handout which you can send home to them to explain what this self-control programme is, what it aims to achieve and how they can help their child develop good self-control skills. It is by no means essential that you use this handout, but it is included here in case you wish to do so.

The second section of this book (chapter five) contains the details of the programme itself. This programme is designed to be carried out over an eight-week period, and it consists of two introductory sessions followed by sixteen thirty-minute game sessions (to be conducted at a rate of two per week). However, this programme is very flexible, so do not worry if you cannot find the time to do it all in a single eight-week block. In fact, even if all you manage to cover are the two introductory sessions, your students will most likely still benefit from it. This is because these introductory sessions will help your students understand what self-control is and why it is important that they learn good self-control skills. This is based on the mind-model developed by Professor Steve Peters (author of *The Chimp Paradox*, a book that is well worth reading, if you have the time to spare). The game sessions involve a series of simple, physical games which have been specifically designed to help children use and develop their self-control skills. These sessions can be integrated into typical primary PE classes and so should not require you to find extra time to complete them.

The third section of this book (chapters six to eight) provides you with additional information about how you can encourage your students to come up with their own self-control development games, how you can help them track of how their self-control skills are developing, and how you can integrate self-control development training into other parts of your teaching.

The final section of this book (chapter nine) provides some recommendations for additional reading about self-control and its importance as a life skill for children (and adults). While you may find these useful, please do not feel that you need to read these materials unless you are particularly interested in them.

---- *Chapter Two* ----
What Is Self-Control And Why Is It Important For Children To Learn This Life Skill?

Self-control is the ability to think through all the consequences of your actions in advance and make a decision that will result in the best possible long-term outcome for you as an individual. In this respect, self-control is the opposite of impulsiveness, and you can think of self-control as the ability to forego a small, instantaneous reward now for a much better reward in the future. For this reason, self-control is also known as the ability to delay gratification.

Why Is Self Control Important?

Self-control is important because it is the key to developing self-motivation, persistence, long-term planning, academic achievement and good financial management. The level of self-control, or delayed gratification, can be measured using something called the marshmallow test. In this test, a child is left alone in a room with a desirable treat, such as a marshmallow, and they are told that if they manage to resist eating it before the tester returns, they will get two instead of one. This may seem like a trivial test, but the ability to delay gratification, as measured by this test, is one of the strongest and best predictors of the level of success a child will go on to achieve in their adult lives. Specifically, the stronger the ability to delay gratification at a young age, the greater the likelihood of success in adult life. This is true across a wide range of measures, and good self-control skills in children have been found to lead to adults who are better able to maintain high quality personal relationships, less likely to become obese, less likely to have problems with drugs or alcohol, who will go further in education, and who will earn more money. In short, children with good self-control skills are much more likely to grow into happy, successful adults than those who have poor self-control skills.

What Age Should Children Start Developing Self-Control?

The ability to exert self-control and delay gratification is not innate. Instead, it is a behaviour that we learn. Self-control should start to appear around the age of three, and while children will vary greatly for any given age, the greatest changes in the ability to delay gratification occur between the ages of three and seven. The better the self-control skills that a child has on entering school, the better they will most likely do, so it is a good idea to ensure that this life skill is as developed as possible at as early a stage as possible.

Self-Control And Education

Unfortunately, few young children get specific training to improve their levels of self-control. Instead, they are left to develop it on their own. While this approach may work for children who grow up in relatively stable households where good self-control behaviours are regularly on display, are encouraged and are rewarded, it leaves children who grow up in less stable households, where good self-control behaviours are not commonly exhibited, encouraged or rewarded, with few opportunities to develop this critical life skill at an appropriate stage in their development. This, in turn, means that these children enter school with poorly developed self-control and they have little ability to delay gratification, concentrate for even short periods of time without becoming distracted or to control their impulses and emotions. This not only damages their own ability to learn, it also disrupts the learning of other students in the same classroom, and it can have life-long consequences for individual children. As a result, it would be beneficial if all children received a specific course of self-control development training as early as possible in their school career. This will do no harm to those children who already have good self-control skills, and it has the potential to greatly increase the self-control skills of those children in whom it is poorly developed, with life-long positive consequences. In addition, as well as helping individual children, raising the level of self-control skills of those students where it is poorest will benefit both the teacher and the rest of their class as there will be fewer disruptions and distractions caused by those individual children with poorly developed self-control skills.

This book aims to help address this issue by providing a simple, but effective, programme which can be implemented in primary classrooms to help all children understand, practice and develop their self-control skills, and raise the levels of self-control in children where, for whatever reason, this skill is poorly developed. This will increase the chances of these children achieving a better educational outcome not only in their first few years of school, but throughout their time in education. In addition, it will increase the chances of them growing into happy and successful adults. This programme can be implemented at any age within primary schools, but it will have the greatest benefits when it is applied in primary two, three or four. This is because children in these age classes are old enough to understand what self-control is and why it is important, but young enough for their self-control skills to still be easily malleable

---- *Chapter Three* ----
How Does This Programme Help Develop Good Self-Control Skills?

There are four elements to developing good self-control skills. These are having a good working memory, practising self-control, having a good adult self-control role-model, and learning that exhibiting self-control is worthwhile. This programme specifically targets the first two of these elements and aims to help expand the working memory of your students and give them the opportunity to practice using self-control in a fun and enjoyable environment. The reason that it is important to enhance their working memories is that self-control requires a child to be able to hold several points of view in their minds at the same time and assess which one of them will give the best long-term benefits. If a child does not have a sufficiently developed working memory, they will be unable to do this.

Both working memory and self-control can be enhanced by regularly playing games that require the use of both of these elements. Such games need to have three criteria: The need to require the children playing it to remember more than one rule; they need to have rules that change as the game is played; and these changes need to happen on a non-predictable basis. When a game has all three of these criteria, it requires the child to be continually recalling the rules, remembering which rules to apply when, to be continually paying attention, and to think before they act. It is by requiring them to do all these things at once that this type of game helps develop working memory and allows children to practice using self-control.

Luckily, it is surprisingly easy to design simple games that fulfil all three of these criteria, and such games form the basis of this programme. The games used in it can be divided into three basic types: Rule-switching games; location-based rules games and list-following games. Rule-switching games are ones like *Red Light-Green Light* (where the children playing it run around when they hear the command 'Green Light' and stop when they hear the command 'Red Light' – see page twenty-six) that offer two commands each with its own specific response. Playing games like this requires listening, but little concentration, working memory or self-control. However, by introducing a 'Switch' command into such games (this switches what happens whenever either of the two original commands are issued), suddenly the children have to concentrate a lot more, use more working memory and use more self-control, and this helps develop all of these areas. Children also enjoy the confusion created by this additional switching element.

Location-based rules games, such as *Base Camp*, require different things to be done at different locations, and require the children to remember what they need to do at each one (see page thirty for full details of this game). If the locations are randomly interspersed with each other (for example, if they are defined by different coloured hula hoops laid out randomly on the floor), then the children playing it cannot simply copy their neighbours and this means that they need to put in a lot more effort to remember what action they need to do when they arrive at each type of location. This, in turn, helps them to develop their working memory. This is particularly true if the locations they will use are decided on a random basis and are not defined in advance.

List-following games, such as *Follow The Leader*, require children to listen to an entire list of commands before completing them in the order they were given (see page thirty-three for full details of this game). This requires children to hold the full list of commands in the correct order in their working memory before they act. This is a great way to enhance working memory and to practice thinking before you act.

This programme not only uses all three of these types of games, but it mixes them up and continually adds new elements. This means that while the children will quickly become familiar with the basic rules behind these games, they will have to be continually focussing during each and every session to ensure that they are playing them correctly. In addition, by requiring the children themselves to start selecting the games they will play and even inventing their own variations on these basic game types, it increases engagement and encourages them to take ownership of this self-control development programme.

While the games in this programme will help enhance working memory and give children practice in exhibiting self-control, they do not cover the remaining two elements of developing good self-control skills (having a good adult model for self-control and learning that exhibiting self-control is worthwhile). If these elements can also be provided in conjunction with this programme, it will further increase its effectiveness. For this reason, a four-page handout is provided in chapter four which can be given to parents to provide them with information on how they can help with these two elements. However, it is an unfortunate reality that the children who are likely to benefit most from enhancing their self-control skills are also those who are most likely to come from households where it is least likely to be in evidence. As a result, it is important that you, as their teacher, also try to provide as much of these additional elements as you can.

In particular, it has been shown that children who do not trust the adults in their lives to actually give them promised future rewards are the ones who will generally have poor self-control skills. This is because they have learned that future promised rewards are unlikely to be delivered so they might as well take whatever is on offer now (as it is a certainty that they will actually get it). A child only needs to be disappointed in this way a small number of times to learn that self-control and delayed gratification are not worthwhile. This means that it is essential that you always keep your word with your students, and that you always follow up on any promises of rewards that you make. In addition, it is important that you never remove promised rewards earned for displaying and using self-control skills as punishments for other, unrelated, actions. Information and advice on how you can integrate the demonstration of these additional elements into the rest of your teaching are provided in chapter eight.

---- Chapter Four ----
What To Tell Parents/Carers About The Importance Of Self-Control Development And The Contents Of This Programme

This programme will have the greatest impact on individual students if the mental elements it aims to enhance, such as working memory, and the self-control skills it aims to develop are integrated into other elements of your teaching (see chapter eight) and into your students' lives beyond school. Thus, while completing this programme will hopefully benefit your students regardless of any additional external inputs, it will have a greater impact if parents, carers and other key adults in the lives of your students both understand the importance of self-control and contribute towards its development.

On the next four pages, you will find a set of handouts that you can photocopy and give to parents/carers with the aim of helping them understand why self-control is an important skill for their child to learn, and how they can help contribute to its development. Not all parents/carers will be willing to do this, and some may well disagree with it, but it is still beneficial that they are provided with this information. However, frustrating as it may be, it will be up to them to decide if they wish to act on this information, or to ignore it.

Self-Control Development Training
Information For Parents/Carers

Over the next few weeks, as part of their normal classroom activities, your child will take part in a programme that will aim to develop their self-control skills. Self-control is the ability to think through all the consequences of your actions in advance and make a decision which will result in the best possible long-term outcome for you as an individual. In this respect, self-control is the opposite of impulsiveness, and you can think of self-control as the ability to forego a small instantaneous reward now for a much better reward in the future. For this reason, it is also known as the ability to delay gratification.

Self-control is an important skill for your child to develop because it has been found that children who develop good self-control behaviours at a young age have a greater chance of growing into happy and successful adults. In fact, good self-control skills in children have been found to be related to better academic performance in both primary and secondary school, higher earnings as adults, more responsible financial behaviours, better personal relationships and a reduced likelihood of developing dependencies on alcohol and drugs.

The programme that your child will be taking part in has been specifically designed for primary-aged children and is based on the results of a number of studies that have shown that this type of training can enhance a child's working memory and self-control.

What Does This Programme Involve?

This programme is divided into two parts. The first part involves two introductory sessions where your child will learn about what self-control is and why it is beneficial for them to use it to ensure they respond appropriately to different situations they may encounter. They also learn that there is an innate part of all of our brains that makes us act impulsively, even when it is not appropriate. This is referred to as a child's inner cheeky chimp. Referring to it in this way helps children visualise it in a fun and amusing way, and it also helps them to identify when this part of their brain is causing them to react inappropriately in any given situation. This is because they learn to segregate which thought patterns and behaviours are the result of the rational, thinking parts of their brains, and which are the results of the impulsive, unthinking parts. This, in turn, helps them learn to control their impulses in situations where it would be inappropriate to let them dictate their thinking and behaviour.

The second part of this programme involves playing a number of physical games that require children to use their working memory and their self-control.

This allows them to exercise these skills in a fun way, and by doing this, it helps reinforce and strengthen them.

How Can You Help?

While this programme, on its own, should have a beneficial impact on your child's self control skills, these benefits will be enhanced if the skills they learn are also reinforced outside of school. As a result, we would like you, as the important adults in your child's life, to get as involved as possible in developing you child's self-control skills. We realise that you are busy and that you may not have a huge amount of free time to devote to this, but anything you can fit in will be of benefit, even if it only lasts for a few minutes at a time. Helping your child develop their self-control skills can be as simple as using the journey to and from school to play games that help enhance working memory and develop self-control skills or having a discussion with them about why self-control is important, talking through examples of situations where it is important to apply self-control and what are appropriate responses to specific situations that involve the use of self-control.

There are six basic ways that the adults in a child's life can help them enhance their working memory and help them develop good self-control skills. These are:

1. **Modelling:** One of the main ways that children learn important life skills is by observing how the adults in their lives behave and react. Thus, if children observe adults using self-control in an appropriate way on a regular basis, they will learn that this is how they, too, should behave. This means that it is important that, as far as is possible, the adults in a child's life model good self-control behaviours. This can include resisting giving in to temptations, avoiding responding aggressively in social interactions and avoiding inappropriate impulsive behaviours. As a result, the more you model good self-control behaviour for your child, the greater the likelihood that they will follow your example and develop good self-control behaviours themselves. Of course, we all lose control occasionally and act irrationally or impulsively. If you find that you do this in front of your child, it is important that you don't try to cover it up or pretend it didn't happen. Instead, be open about it. Admit that everyone can struggle with self-control from time to time and that you responded inappropriately to a particular situation. In addition, explain how exhibiting self-control would have resulted in a more positive outcome for you, how it would have been better for you to react, and that you will try harder to react more appropriately in the future. This will help your child learn a positive lesson from such events, rather than learning that losing self-control is an acceptable behaviour.

2. **Playing Games:** Play is one of the best ways for children (and adults) to learn. This is why the self-control development programme your child will be completing in school is primarily based around using games to help children enhance their working memories and develop their self-control skills. If this play element can be extended beyond school, it will greatly increase the likelihood that they will develop good self-control skills. As a result, if you have the time, it will be beneficial to your child if you regularly play games that will help them develop their working memories and their self-control skills. These games can include not only physical games, like the ones they will do at school as part of this programme, but also mental games that require children to remember lists of items (such as *The President's Cat*), card games that require self-control and penalise impulsive behaviour (such as *Pairs* and *Snap*) and even smart phone/tablet apps (such as *Classic Simon*). Details of these, and other, games can be found at the end of this handout.

3. **Practice:** Children will only develop good self-control skills if they are given the opportunity to practice using them on a regular basis. As a result, the more opportunities you give your child to practice their self-control skills, the more developed they will become. While it can be incredibly frustrating to watch your child struggle with their self-control, especially if they keep failing to use it appropriately, it is still important to give them these opportunities. If they fail, try to resist criticising their failures and instead encourage them to learn from the experience and try again another time.

4. **Positive And Appropriate Praise:** Praise is an incredibly powerful tool, and when used appropriately, it can go a long way to helping shape a child's behaviour. Appropriate praise has to be specific, positive and aimed an encouraging a child to repeat a desirable behaviour rather than focussing on an innate character trait. This can be difficult for many people to do, but a few small changes to the way that praise is given can greatly enhance its beneficial effects. Specifically, make sure that you praise the effort they put in, and not just the results, and also that you praise learned behaviours and not innate character traits. You can find more information about how to positively praise a child at *www.howtoraiseahappygenius.com/parental-skill-seven-ways-to-positively-praise-your-child/*.

5. **Discussion:** Children can learn a huge amount from discussions with the adults in their lives. In particular, they can learn about appropriate and inappropriate behaviours, which situations they need to exhibit good self-control in, and which responses are acceptable and which are not. Such discussions need to be non-judgemental and not focussed on mistakes that a child may have made in the past. Instead, use examples from books they have read, films they have watched, sports they like or even from your own lives. This last type of example

can be particularly instructive, especially if you are open about mistakes you have made, how acting without self-control caused you problems and how you could have got a better outcome with a more rational, controlled response.

6. Trust: It has been shown that children who do not trust the adults in their lives to actually give them promised future rewards will generally develop poor self-control skills. This is because they have learned that future promised rewards are unlikely to be delivered so they might as well take what is on offer now (as it is a certainty that they will actually get it). Unfortunately, a child only needs to be disappointed in this way a small number of times to learn that self-control is not worth the effort. This means that, as far as possible, it is essential that you always keep your word with your child and that you always follow up on promises of rewards that you make (and that you never remove promised rewards for showing good self-control and delayed gratification as punishments for other actions).

Games You Can Play With Your Child To Help Them Develop Their Working Memory And Self-Control

Below are a list of games which you can play with your child that will help to enhance their working memory and develop their self-control skills. These games have the common theme that the child need to remember rules or lists of items and think before they do anything to ensure that they are acting appropriately.

Red Light - Green Light - Switch: This game is very simple, but very effective, and it is one of the first games your child will play as part of the self-control development programme they are completing at school. When you call out "Green Light" your child can move around, but when you call out "Red Light", they must freeze instantly and stay frozen until you say "Green Light" again. At random intervals you call out "Switch", and the meaning of each command is switched over. This makes the game more mentally taxing, as well as more fun for your child.

Simon Says Switch: Again, this is one of the first games your child will play as part of the self-control development programme they are completing at school. You call out commands, and your child has to follow them, but only when you precede a command by the words "Simon Says". The game is over when they do a command when they shouldn't, or don't do a command when they should. Again, the effectiveness of this game can be enhanced by switching the rules around every now and then so that the child has to follow commands which aren't preceded by the phrase "Simon Says", and ignore commands that are. This is a game that you can play outside, in the house, or even in the car (but make sure it doesn't affect your concentration if you are driving).

The Observation Game: While the previous two games were about following rules and resisting acting when you need to, this game is about increasing working memory. Find a small tray and place as diverse a range of household objects on it as you can find. Aim to have between fifteen and twenty objects, and make sure that each object can be clearly seen and does not overlap with any others. Cover the tray and put it in front of your child. Remove the cover and tell them they have twenty seconds to remember as many of the objects as they can. Once the twenty seconds are up, cover the tray and ask your child to tell you every object they can remember. If you are playing with several children, they can take it in turns to say an object, with each one dropping out when they cannot correctly name an object on the tray.

The President's Cat: While *The Observation Game* requires some preparation and cannot easily be played on the move, *The President's Cat* can be played anywhere and at any time. This game is played by coming up with a list of attributes for the president's cat. The first must start with A, the second with B and so on through the alphabet. Start by saying "The President's cat is a … cat" (where you add in an attribute beginning with A into the space provided). Your child goes next, and repeats this phrase and the first attribute before adding their own beginning with B. This continues with you each taking turns until someone misses a previously mentioned attribute in the list. Played regularly, this will help to increase working memory and focus, both of which contribute to the development of good self-control skills.

Simon: *Simon* is a simple electronic game you may well remember from your own childhood. It flashes a sequence of lights that you have to remember and copy in order to move onto the next level. At each level, the sequence gets longer and will continue until a mistake is made. This can be purchased as a stand-alone game. However, you can also find and download free apps, such as *Classic Simon*, that allow you to play *Simon* on most tablets and smart phones.

Card games: Traditional card games like *Snap* and *Pairs* can help enhance your child's working memory and self-control, as can playing more modern games like *Uno*. Even games like *Top Trumps* can be adapted for improving these elements. For example, in traditional *Top Trumps*, the card with the largest value in a given category is the winner. However, you can add in a rule-switching element into this by randomly changing whether it is the card with the highest or the lowest value that will win any given round. Other good card games for enhancing working memory include *Blink* and *Dobble*.

---- *Chapter Five* ----
The Self-Control Development Programme

This programme consists of two introductory sessions followed by up to sixteen half-hour game sessions that are ideally run over a period of eight weeks (but see below for information about how to adapt it if you cannot fit the entire course into your class timetable). While it might seem that this is too little to have any significant long-term impacts, it has been shown that this is sufficient to raise the level of self-control in children who do not have good self-control skills at the start of such a programme. During each of these sessions, the children engage in a series of games which not only require them to follow instructions, but that also require them to think about which instructions they need to follow at any given moment. The key element of these games is that the rules they need to follow are constantly changing, meaning they have to use their working memory and think before they act to ensure that they follow the right instructions at the right time. In the first session, these games are relatively simply and straight forward, but as the sessions continue, they become more complex. This helps children increase the capacity of their working memory, and this, in turn, increases their ability to assess and control their own behaviours, which is the basis of self-control.

Since these games all involve being very active, they can be conducted during PE classes. This can make it easier to implement this programme alongside your normal teaching requirements. However, if you find that you do not have the time to complete this course in a single eight-week period, do not worry too much. After you have done the two introductory sessions, feel free to adapt the remaining part of the programme to fit the time that you have available for it. This can include spreading them out over a longer period or doing fewer sessions. Similarly, you can shorten the individual sessions by reducing the time that you spend on each game or by dropping an individual game from it. Finally, even if you do not have time to do any of the game sessions, simply doing the two introductory sessions is likely to prove beneficial for your students. This is because these sessions will help them understand what self-control is, why it is important and how they can work towards improving their self-control skills. In addition, these introductory sessions alone are sufficient to allow you to introduce elements of self-control development into other parts of your teaching to reinforce the lessons your students have learned from them (see chapter eight for more information on how you can do this), and any of these elements that you can introduce into your classroom will be benefit your students.

Introductory Session One: Explaining Self-Control To Children

Before you start working on this programme with your class, you need to explain to your students what self-control is and why it is important. This can be done using a simplified version of the mind management model developed by Professor Steve Peters. In this model, the child's brain can be pictured as having two parts to it: a part that acts like a rational human being, and a part that acts like a cheeky chimpanzee. The human part is the bit that thinks before they act, while the chimp part is the bit that acts before they think, and because the chimp part does this when it is in control, children often end up doing things that get them into trouble. The idea of self-control development training is to give the human part of their brains the tools to help them control their chimp part when they need to do so. This does not mean that they cannot let the chimp part of their brain out to play every now and then, just that it will help them keep control of it at times when it is not appropriate for it to be in charge of their behaviours.

This can be explained to your students using the exercise sheets that you will find on the following three pages. These worksheets aim to help your students understand that there is a part of their brain which can lead them to act impulsively (referred to as the cheeky chimp part) and that while it is okay to let this part of their brain control their behaviours sometimes, at others it will get them into trouble. As a result, they will benefit if they learn how and when to control this part of their brain using self-control skills.

To use these worksheets, start by handing out the first sheet and getting your students to fill in their name and draw a picture of themselves in the top section. Next, introduce them to the idea that their behaviours are controlled by their brains and that different parts of their brain may wish them to act in different ways even in the same situation. The human part will want them to act thoughtfully and responsibly, while the cheeky chimp part will want them to act impulsively and this can lead to them getting into trouble if it results in them doing something inappropriate for a given situation.

You can now move onto the second worksheet. Here, the students get to draw a picture of what they imagine the cheeky chimp part of their brains might look like if it were a real chimpanzee, and also to give it a name of their choosing. This helps them personalise it and also provides them with a way of addressing it as a concrete entity rather than as an invisible concept.

My name is _____

I look like this:
(Draw a picture of yourself here)

You might not know it by looking at me, but I have a cheeky chimpanzee in my head.

Don't worry, it is not a real cheeky chimpanzee. It is just a part of my brain that likes to make me act like one.

Sometimes this is okay, but sometimes it is not and this can get me into trouble.

This is what I think my cheeky chimp looks like this:

(Draw a picture of what you think your cheeky chimp looks like here)

Its name is _____

It is up to me, and not my cheeky chimp, to decide when it is okay for it to come out to play.

To do this, I need to try to think before I act, and use my self-control skills to stop my cheeky chimp from taking over the rest of my brain.

My name is _____ My Cheeky Chimp's Name is _____

It is in my power to learn how to control the cheeky chimp part of my brain. It is also in my best interest to learn how to do this.

These are some situations where I need to try to control my cheeky chimp:

These are some situations where it is okay to let my cheeky chimp come out to play:

1. _____
2. _____
3. _____
4. _____
5. _____

1. _____
2. _____
3. _____
4. _____
5. _____

The more often I try to control my cheeky chimp when I need to (even if I don't always succeed), the better I will get at doing it.

Once your students have finished drawing what they imagine their inner chimps look like, ask them to think of situations where it would be appropriate to act like a cheeky chimpanzee. This might include while playing in the playground during the mid-morning break or playing in the park with friends after school. Listen to their suggestions and write them on a whiteboard at the front of the class.

Next, ask your students to think of situations where acting like a cheeky chimp is likely to get them into trouble (they will probably find this a lot easier to do). This might be while they are working in class, while they are in the dinner hall having lunch or when they are at the shops with their parents. Again, listen to their suggestions and write them down on a whiteboard at the front of the class.

If you wish, you can turn these two sets of situations into a poster that you can put on your classroom wall. It can then act as a continual reminder of examples of situations where it is acceptable for children to act like a cheeky chimp and when it is not.

Once you have done this, you can move onto the third worksheet. Start by getting them to fill out their name and the name they have given to their cheeky chimp at the top of the page. Next, you can explain to them that it is within their powers to learn how to control the cheeky chimp part of their brains and that it is in their best interest to do this as they will get into trouble less frequently if they do so. This is important to emphasise as children need to understand that their self-control skills are not a fixed part of their personalities, but instead are something which they can develop and improve.

Now, ask your students to come up with different situations they have encountered in their lives, or that they can think up, and then ask them to classify whether these are situations where they need to try to control their cheeky chimp, or whether it would be okay to let their cheeky chimp come out and play. This will help them learn to identify situations where they need to apply self-control to rein in their naturally impulsive behaviours, and situations where it is okay to give into such impulses. These situations can be linked back to the earlier ones about when it is okay to act like a cheeky chimp and when doing so might get them into trouble. However, it is worth emphasising the difference between these two ways of looking at them. In the first way, they were simply considering whether certain behaviours would get them into trouble. In the second, they are taking ownership of the need to control their impulses in certain situations. Once you have come up with a list of situations as a class, ask your students to write down examples of five situations where they need to try to control their cheeky chimp and five examples of situations where it is okay to let their cheeky chimps come out to play.

Finally, once your students have finished their two lists, you can emphasise to them that the more often they try to control the cheeky chimp part of their brains (even if they don't always succeed), the better they will get at doing it. It should be emphasised at this point that the most important element here is that they try to do this as frequently as possible and not necessarily that they always succeed. This will prevent them from becoming discouraged and giving up if they do not manage to control the cheeky chimp part of their brains right away, or on every possible occasion.

Introductory Session Two: Explaining To Children That There Are Times When It Is Important To Listen To What Their Inner Chimp Is Telling Them

Once your students understand the basics of the cheeky chimp mind management model, how they can use it to help them understand what self-control is and why it is important, it is essential that you also explain to them that there are times when it is important to the listen to what their inner chimp is telling them.

To do this, you can explain that one of the reasons we have an inner cheeky chimp is that it can help protect us. The trouble is that sometimes our cheeky chimps have a tendency to over-react, and at others, they will read a situation completely wrong and suggest we do things we really should not be doing. This means we need to learn to tell when we need to listen to our inner chimpanzees in order to protect ourselves, when it is over-reacting to a particular situation and we need to learn to bring it under control, and when it is reading a situation completely wrongly and is telling us to do something that is totally inappropriate. As a result, it is important that students learn to differentiate between these types of situations and to act accordingly. For example, if their inner chimp is telling them that an adult's behaviour towards them is inappropriate (such as if they are being touched in a way that makes them feel uncomfortable), it is really important that they know not to over-rule what their chimp is telling them and that it is okay to tell the adult to stop. Similarly, there may be times when other children, especially older children, are encouraging them to do things that their inner chimp is telling them are wrong or that could get them into trouble. Again, it is important that these feelings are not over-ruled.

The best way to explain to your students when they should listen to what their inner cheeky chimps are telling them, and when they should exercise self-control is by using an exercise called *Always, Sometimes, Never*. In this exercise, you will provide your students with six very simple scenarios and ask them to decide whether, in each one, they should always listen to what they inner cheeky chimp is telling them, whether they should only listen to it if the situation is appropriate, or whether they should never listen to it. These scenarios, along with the most appropriate answer for each one (and explanations of why this is the case), are provided below.

To start this exercise, hand out a copy of the worksheet provided on page twenty-four to each student. Explain to them that you are going to give them six different situations followed by an example of what their cheeky chimp might tell them they should do in each one. They then need to decide whether they should always listen to their cheeky chimp in such circumstances, sometimes listen to it (depending on the exact circumstances) or never listen to it. Next, designate areas of your classroom to represent each of these three possible options and tell your students that after you have given them a scenario, they need to move to the area that represents the response they think is most appropriate for it. Once they understand what they need to do, read out the first scenario and ask them to move to the area of the classroom that corresponds with how they think they should respond to it. After they have stopped moving around, ask your students to explain why they selected the option they did, and then give them with the most appropriate answer provided for each scenario and get them to fill this in on their worksheet. This should help them understand the thought processes they need to go through in order to assess whether they should listen to their cheeky chimp, or not, in any given situation. It also allows them to see and, and understand, how differently each of them may view the same situation. Repeat this process for the five remaining situations.

Once you have gone through these scenarios with your students, ask them to come up with their own scenarios and discuss whether they should always listen, listen sometimes or never listen to their cheeky chimps. This will help them develop the ability to decide when listening to their inner chimp is appropriate, and when they need to use self-control to over-ride what their cheeky chimp is telling them to do.

The Scenarios

Scenario One - You see a group of children playing a really fun game in the park, and your cheeky chimp is tells you to immediately run over and join in. In this type of situation, should you always listen to your cheeky chimp, listen to it sometimes or never listen to it?

The most appropriate answer here is *Listen Sometimes*. This is because there will be some situations where this is okay to do what their cheeky chimp is suggesting they should do, such as when a child is already in the park playing, while there are other situations where it is not, such as when a child is on the other side of a busy road, or when they have something else that they need to do first. See if your students can come up with other examples of times when you should and shouldn't listen to your cheeky chimp in this situation.

Scenario Two - You see a toy you really want in a shop, but you don't have the money to pay for it. Your cheeky chimp tells you to hide it in your pocket so you can take it home without paying for it. In this type of situation, should you always listen to your cheeky chimp, listen to it sometimes or never listen to it?

The most appropriate answer here is *Never Listen*. This is an example of a situation where a child's cheeky chimp has read it completely wrongly. As a result, if they listened to what their cheeky chimp was telling them, they would end up stealing something, and they could get into a lot of trouble.

Scenario Three - You see a balloon and your cheeky chimp tells you it would be really fun to burst it. In this type of situation, should you always listen to your cheeky chimp, listen to it sometimes or never listen to it?

The most appropriate answer here is *Listen Sometimes*. This is because there will be some situations where this is okay, such as when it is their balloon, while there are other situations where it is not, such if the balloon belongs to someone else. See if your students can come up with other examples of when you should and shouldn't listen to your cheeky chimp in this situation.

Scenario Four - A grown-up asks you to give them a kiss and your cheeky chimp tells you not to do it because it make you feel very uncomfortable. In this type of situation, should you always listen to your cheeky chimp, listen to it sometimes or never listen to it?

The most appropriate answer here is *Always Listen*. This is an example of a situation where the child's cheeky chimp is right and is trying to protect them. This is because a child should always be in charge of who kisses them, and they have the right to tell someone not to kiss them if they don't want them to. In situations like this, where someone is trying to do something with a child's body that makes them feel uncomfortable, they should always listen to what their cheeky chimp is telling them.

Scenario Five - You see a glass bottle in the street, and your cheeky chimp tells you kick it over to see what happens. In this type of situation, should you always listen to your cheeky chimp, listen to it sometimes or never listen to it?

The most appropriate answer here is *Never Listen*. This is an example of a situation where the child's cheeky chimp has read it completely wrongly. While it may be fun to kick the bottle over, it is not an appropriate thing to do. This is because it could break and leave broken glass over the ground which could injury another child or an animal.

Scenario Six - An older child dares you to do something, but your cheeky chimp tells you not to do it because it could get you into trouble. The older child calls you a baby for not wanting to do it. In this type of situation,

should you always listen to your cheeky chimp, listen to it sometimes or never listen to it?

The most appropriate answer here is *Always Listen*. This is an example of a situation where a child's cheeky chimp is right and is trying to protect them. This is because they shouldn't let anyone else manipulate or bully them into doing something that their inner chimp is telling them is wrong.

When Is It Important To Listen To My Cheeky Chimp?

My name is _____ My cheeky chimp's name is _____

While sometimes my cheeky chimp can get me into trouble if I don't try to control it, there are other times when it is giving me really important advice that I need to listen to.

I can tell the difference between these situations by thinking about what my cheeky chimp is telling me to do, and why it is doing this.

What Your Cheeky Chimp Is Telling You To Do In Each Situation	Always Listen	Listen Sometimes	Never Listen
1. Run and play with the other children			
2. Hide the toy in your pocket so you can take it home.			
3. Burst the balloon.			
4. Don't give the grown-up a kiss if it makes you feel uncomfortable.			
5. Kick the bottle over to see what happens.			
6. Don't do what the older child is trying to get you to do.			

Explaining To Your Students What They Will Learn During This Self-Control Development Programme

At the end of these introductory sessions, it is important to explain to your students what the rest of this programme involves. You can do this by explaining to them that, over the next few weeks, they will be playing a series of games that will help them develop their self-control skills and that this will help them control the part of their brain that wants them to act like a cheeky chimp when it is not appropriate to do so. However, it is important that you also highlight that different children develop these self-control skills at different ages and at different rates, and that they shouldn't get disheartened if other children in the class appear to be doing better than they are, especially at first. Instead, they should concentrate on examining how their own self-control skills are changing over time, and whether they are improving. You should also remind them that self-control abilities are not fixed, but are something they can always improve as long as they keep trying to do so. This both helps prime your students' brains to understand what they will be doing, and to provide them with a framework to assess how well they are doing that does not solely rely on comparisons with others. This is a form of wise psychological intervention that helps each child to understand that they are not necessarily expected to be as good as everyone else right away, and that as long as they keep trying they will get there in the end.

Details of the sixteen thirty-minute game-playing sessions that constitute the main part of this programme are provided on the following pages.

Week One

Session One

The emphasis for session one is on listening to and following instructions, and consists of three games, each of which last approximately ten minutes. This session is designed to provide a basic introduction to the types of games that will be played throughout these sessions. Older children may find these games too basic, and if they do, feel free to skip this session and move onto session two, which introduces more complex versions of these games. To assess whether you should skip this session or not, start by playing the first game (*Red Light-Green Light*), and if your students are clearly finding it too simple, move onto the first game of session two (*Red Light-Green Light-Switch*) and complete session two instead.

Game One: Red Light-Green Light – For this game, tell your students that they need to run around whenever the light is green, but they must freeze as soon as the light turns red. Start the session by shouting "Green Light", at which point the children can start running around. After about twenty seconds, shout "Red Light", at which point the children must freeze. You can then alternates between shouting "Red Light" and "Green Light" at intervals between five and fifteen seconds, and your students have to respond appropriately to each instruction given.

Game Two: Dancing Fast, Dancing Slow – For this game, you need to clap out a rhythm. When the rhythm is fast, your students need to dance or move fast, when it is slow they need to dance or move slowly. At random intervals of between ten and twenty seconds, change the rhythm so that your students need to change how they are dancing or moving.

Game Three: Spots – In this game, a number of red and blue coloured circles are placed on the ground, with enough of each colour for every child to stand on one. Tell your students that when they hear the name of a colour, they need to find a spot of that colour and stand on it (with only one child allowed on each circle). Once you are sure they understand what they need to do, tell them they can start running around. After about ten seconds, shout out a colour of your choice. Once every child is standing on an appropriately coloured circle, you can instruct them to start running around again. This is repeated for approximately ten minutes. **Note:** If you have children in your class who cannot easily discriminate between red and blue, use other colour combinations, or use high-contrast black and white patterns like stripes and spots, rather than colours.

Session Two

The emphasis for session two is on learning to think about the instructions given during the games and interpreting them according to a specific set of rules. It consists of the same three games introduced in session one, but for each one, a new switch command is introduced, which means the children have to do the opposite of any instructions they hear. As before, each game lasts approximately ten minutes.

Note: When playing these games, you may well find that when you are using the switch commands, you get confused as to exactly what your students are meant to be doing at any particular time. An easy way to keep track of this is to close one hand into a fist when you give your first switch command, open it when you give the second, close it again on the third and so on. If you do this correctly, you will know that whenever your fist is closed, your students need to be doing the opposite of your commands (e.g. running around on hearing the command "Red Light"), and when it is open, they need to be following the commands themselves (e.g. stopping on the command "Red Light").

Game One: Red Light-Green Light-Switch – In this game, your students need to run around whenever the light is green, but they must freeze as soon as the light turns red (these are the same rules used for this game in session one). However, when they hear the world "Switch", they must then run around when the light is red and stop when it is green. When they hear the word "Switch" again, they must go back to the original instructions, and so on. Start this session by shouting "Green Light", at which point your students can start running around. After about ten seconds, shout "Red Light", at which point they must freeze. You can then alternates between shouting "Red Light" and "Green Light" at intervals between five and fifteen seconds, with your students responding accordingly to the instruction given. About once a minute, shouts 'Switch" at which point your students must start doing the opposite of what they were previously doing when then hear the words "Red Light" and "Green Light".

Game Two: Dancing Fast, Dancing Slow, Switch – For this game, you need to clap out a rhythm. When the rhythm is fast, your students need to dance or move fast, when it is slow, they must dance or move slowly. The speed of the rhythm is changed at random intervals of between ten and thirty seconds for the duration of the game. After a minute, shout "Switch". At this point, your students must dance or move fast when they hear the slow rhythm and dance or move slow when they hear the fast rhythm. This continues with your students being asked to switch between matching the rhythm or doing the opposite whenever they hear the word "Switch".

27

Game Three: Spots Switch – In this game, a number of red and blue coloured circles are placed on the ground, with enough of each colour for every child to stand on one. Tell your students that when they hear the name of a colour, they need to find a spot of that colour and stand on it (with only one child allowed on each circle). Once you are sure they understand what they need to do, tell them they can start running around. After about ten seconds, shout out a colour of your choice. Once every child is standing on an appropriately coloured circle, you can tell your students to start running around again. As with the previous games in this session, about once a minute you should shout "Switch" while your students are running around, at which point they need to change between standing on a circle of the next colour shouted out to standing on a circle of the opposite colour, depending on what they had previously been doing. As in session one, if you have children in your class who cannot easily discriminate between red and blue, use other colour combinations, or use high-contrast black and white patterns like stripes and spots, rather than colours.

After five minutes, a competitive element is introduced, where any student who stands on an incorrectly-coloured circle, or who takes too long to find a circle of the right colour to stand in, is eliminated. As the game progresses, you should increase the frequency of the switch command to make it more difficult for your students to remember what colour of circle they should be aiming to find and stand on when a colour is called out. The aim of this competitive element is not to see who wins, but to see how many rounds each individual child can last for. This gives a baseline for measuring their improvements across later sessions. The number of rounds each child successfully completes should be recorded and written on their own personal self-control development handout so that can track how their self-control is developing (see chapter seven). You should aim to reach a point in this assessment part of the session where the instructions are too complicated for any child to successfully follow. This can be done by increasing the number of switch commands issued while your students are running around, to make it more difficult for them to remember what colour of circle they should be aiming to find and stand on when a colour is called out.

Week Two

Session Three

Game One: Red Light-Green Light-Switch – This is the same game as played in session two and the aim here is to provide your students with a refresher of the listening and self-control skills that will be used in this session using a familiar game.

Game Two: Forwards-Backwards-Switch – This is a new game to help ensure that your students further develop their listening and self-control skills by applying them to a new situation. In this game, they start by walking forwards when your give the command "Forwards" and backwards when you give the command "Backwards". When you say the command "Switch", they then need to walk backwards when you say the command "Forwards" and forwards when you say the command "Backwards". Your students then continue swapping between doing as the command instructs and doing the opposite whenever you say the command to "Switch". You should give a command of forwards or backwards at random intervals of between about five and fifteen seconds, and the switch command at random intervals between about twenty and forty-five seconds.

Game Three: Simon Says Switch – This game starts by following the standard rules for *Simon Says*, where your students need to only obey instructions which are preceded by the phrase "Simon Says". However, after approximately one minute, you call out "Simon Says Switch", at which point your students need to only obey the commands which are not preceded by the command "Simon Says". After a few minutes, issue the command "Switch" again to the original mode of play. You can then carry on switching between these two modes of play at random intervals as the game continues. After five minutes, a competitive element is introduced, where any child who obeys a command when they shouldn't, or who doesn't obey a command when they should, is eliminated. As the game progresses, you need to increase the frequency of the switch command to make it more difficult for your students to remember whether they should be obeying orders preceded by nothing or by the phrase "Simon Says". The aim of this competition is not to see who wins, but to see how many rounds each individual child can last for. This can be added to their personal self-control development sheet so they can compare it to the number of rounds they lasted for in session two. As with the assessment for session two, you should gradually increase the complexity of the game until none of the students are capable of following it. This can include trying to catch them out by using the "Simon Says Switch" command when your students are meant to be following commands not preceded by the words "Simon Says" and visa versa.

Session Four

Game One: Forwards-Backwards-Switch – This is the same game as played in session three and the aim here is to provide your students with a refresher of the listening and self-control skills that will be used in this session using a familiar game.

Game Two: Simon Says Switch – Again, this is the same game first played in session three and the aim here is to provide your students with a refresher of the listening and self-control skills that will be used in sessions using a familiar game. However, this is done without the competitive element in the final five minutes as it is meant to act as a refresher rather than for measuring the development of their listening and self-control skills.

Game Three: Base Camp Two – For this game, you will need two different coloured of mats, hula hoops or circles cut out of paper to function as bases. The total number of bases (regardless of their colour) should be equal to the number of children playing the game. Each colour is associated with a different action. For example, a red base might be associated with jumping up and down, and a blue base with spinning round. Start by telling your students (or, better yet, demonstrating) which action is associated with which colour. Then inform them that when you say "Go" they are to start running around, and when you call out "Base Camp" they need to find an unoccupied base and do the action corresponding to the colour of that base. Try this out to make sure they understand what they are meant to be doing. After a few seconds, call out "Go", and they can start running around again. This is then repeated for a period of five minutes. After five minutes, a competitive element is introduced, where anyone who does the wrong action for the colour of the base they end up standing on, or who doesn't do the required action quickly enough, is eliminated. The aim of this competition is not to see who wins, but to see how many rounds each individual child can last for. This can be added to their personal self-control development sheet and compared to the number of rounds they lasted in previous sessions. **Note:** If you have children in your class who cannot easily discriminate between red and blue, use other colour combinations, or use high-contrast black and white patterns like stripes and spots, rather than colours.

Week Three

Session Five

Game One: Red Light-Green Light-Switch – This is the same game first played in session two and the aim here is to provide your students with a refresher of the listening and self-control skills that will be used in this session using a familiar game.

Game Two: Forwards-Backwards-Switch – This is the same game first played in session three and the aim here is to provide your students with a refresher of the listening and self-control skills that will be used in this session using a familiar game.

Game Three: Simon Says Switch – This game starts by following the standard rules for Simon Says, where your students need to only obey instructions which are preceded by the phrase "Simon Says". However, after approximately one minute, you call out "Simon Says Switch", at which point your students need to only obey the commands which are not preceded by the command "Simon Says". After a few minutes, issue the command "Switch" again to the original mode of play. You can then carry on switching between these two modes of play at random intervals as the game continues. After five minutes, a competitive element is introduced, where any child who obeys a command when they shouldn't, or who doesn't obey a command when they should, is eliminated. As the game progresses, you need to increase the frequency of the switch command to make it more difficult for your students to remember whether they should be obeying orders preceded by nothing or by the phrase "Simon Says". The aim of this competition is not to see who wins, but to see how many rounds each individual child can last for. This can be added to their personal self-control development sheet so they can compare it to the number of rounds they lasted for in session four. As before, you should aim to increase the complexity of the game and the switching until it reaches the point where none of your students manage to successfully follow the commands.

Session Six

Game One: Simon Says Switch – This is the same game first played in session three and the aim here is to provide your students with a refresher of the listening and self-control skills that will be used in this sessions using a familiar game. However, this is done without the competitive element in the final five minutes as it is meant to act as a refresher rather than for measuring the development of their listening and self-control skills.

Game Two: Dancing Fast, Dancing Slow, Switch – This is the same game first played in session two and the aim here is to provide your students with a refresher of the listening and self-control skills that will be used in this session using a familiar game.

Game Three: Base Camp Two Switch – This game starts the same as *Base Camp Two* first played in session four. However, After your students have completed the right actions twice, call out "Switch". Under this condition, the blue action switches to the red base, the red action to the blue base. The game then carries on as before, with the switch command being used to change the actions that need to be done on each base. This is then repeated for a period of five minutes. After five minutes, a competitive element is introduced, where anyone who does the wrong action for the colour of the base they end up standing on, or who doesn't do the required action quickly enough, is eliminated. The aim of this competition is not to see who wins, but to see how many rounds each individual child can last for. This can be compared to the number of rounds they lasted in previous sessions. The instructor should aim to reach a point in this assessment part of the session where the instructions are too complicated for any child to successfully follow. This can be done by increasing the number of switch commands issued while your students are running around, to make it more difficult for the children to remember which action they are meant to be completing on which colour.

Week Four

Session Seven

Game One: By this session, your students should be starting to get the hang of the basic elements involved in the different games, and can now be offered a choice of which games they wish to play. Start the session by selecting two previous games of your choice and asking your students which they would like to play. This gives them a feeling of control over the sessions and will increase their engagement with them.

Game Two: Follow The Leader – This is a new game for this session and is slightly different from the previous ones. Have the children line up in rows with their feet together and arms by their sides while you stand in front of them. Tell them that this is the attention position that they need to return to between each action. Next, show them the four actions which are involved in this exercise. These are: 1. Twirl: This action involves spinning round in a single 360 degree turn on the spot with arms held out parallel to the ground and then returning to the attention position; 2. Jump: This action involves jumping once on the spot and then returning to the attention position; 3. Star: This action involves moving their legs and arms out to form a star and than back to standing straight up feet together and arms by their side; 4. Viking Clap: This action involves raising their arms out to the side and then while keeping them straight, raising them further to clap their hands together above their heads and then bringing their arms back down again. Once your students understand what these four actions are, they ready to play the game. Explain to them that you will give them a list of commands, and they must wait until you say "Go" before doing them in the order you said. Start with a single command (like Jump), and then say go. Repeat this for a different command to ensure they understand what they need to do. Next, tell them that you are now going to give them two commands and that they need to remember them, but not carry them out until you say "Go". Now give them two commands (e.g. Jump, Twirl) before saying "Go". Once you have said go, do not remind them of what they were meant to be doing until they have finished. Praise the ones who got it right, and encourage those who didn't to see if they can do it next time. Repeat this, slowly increasing the number of commands until you have reached a point where you are giving them six commands in a row (this can include repeating the same command more than once in a single sequence) before saying "Go". **Note:** If your students find a list of six commands too easy to follow, you can increase the number until you reach the point where they find it challenging to follow.

Game Three: Simon Says Switch – Again, this is the same game first played in session three. After five minutes, a competitive element is introduced, where any child who obeys a command when they shouldn't, or doesn't obey a command when they should, is eliminated. As the game progresses, you should increase the frequency of the switch command to make it more difficult for your students to remember whether they should be obeying orders preceded by nothing or by the phrase 'Simon Says'. The aim of this competition is not to see who wins, but to see how many rounds each individual child can last for. This can be compared to the number of rounds they lasted for in previous sessions.

Session Eight

Game One: Start the session by selecting two previous games of your choice and asking your students which they would like to play. This gives them a feeling of control over the sessions and will increase their engagement with them.

Game Two: For game two, again ask your students to select a preferred game to play.

Game Three: Follow The Leader – This is the same game first played in session seven. However, after five minutes of playing it, introduce a competitive element. As before, remind your students that they are not playing against each other, but that each of them has their own targets and is trying to do better than they have done in earlier sessions. As always, this session is scored based on the number of rounds that each child survives before being eliminated and this can be recorded and compared to the number of rounds they lasted for in previous sessions. For this assessment game, keep gradually increasing the number of commands given before saying go until none of your students manage to successfully remember and follow them all.

Week Five

Session Nine

Game One: Start the session by selecting two previous games of your choice and asking your students which they would like to play. This gives them a feeling of control over the sessions and will increase their engagement with them.

Game Two: For this game, provide your students with a list three games they have played previously and ask them to vote on which game they would like to play next. This increases their feeling of control and will increase their engagement. However, remind your students that if the one they vote for doesn't win this time, that they need to be patient, and it can be played in the next session. This will encourage them to see that just because they don't get something right away, if they are patient, they may still get it in the end.

Game Three: Base Camp Three – For this game, you will need three different colours of mats, hula hoops or circles cut out to paper to function as bases. The total number of bases (regardless of their colours) should be equal to the number of children in the group. Each colour is associated with a different action. For example, a red base might be associated with jumping up and down, a blue base with spinning round and a green base with doing a Viking clap. Tell your students which action is associated with which colour. When you say "Go" they are to start running around, and when you call out "Base Camp" they need to find a base and do the action corresponding to its colour. After a few seconds, call out "Go", and they can start running around again. This is then repeated. After five minutes, a competitive element is introduced, where anyone who does the wrong action for the colour of the base they are standing on, or fails to do the action quickly enough, is eliminated. The aim of this competition is not to see who wins, but to see how many rounds each individual child can last for. This can be added to their personal self-control development sheet and compared to the number of rounds they lasted in previous sessions.

Session Ten

Game One: Start this session with the first of the losing games which were voted on for game two of session nine.

Game Two: For game two of this session, use the second losing game which were voted on for game two of session nine.

Game Three: Follow The Leader – This is the same game first played in session seven. However, after five minutes of playing it, introduce a competitive element. As before, remind your students that they are not playing against each other, but that each of them has their own targets and is trying to do better than they have done in earlier sessions. As always, this session is scored based on the number of rounds that each child survives before being eliminated and this can be recorded and compared to the number of rounds they lasted for in previous sessions.

Week Six

Session Eleven

Game One: For this game, provide your students with a list of three games they have played previously and ask them to vote on which game they would like to play first. This increases their feeling of control and will increase their engagement.

Game Two: For this game, remind your students of the two options that didn't get selected for game one, and ask them to come to a consensus between themselves as to which one they should now play.

Game Three: Simon Says Switch – Again, this is the same game first played in session three. After five minutes, a competitive element is introduced, where any child who obeys a command when they shouldn't, or doesn't obey a command when they should, is eliminated. As the game progresses, you should increase the frequency of the switch command to make it more difficult for your students to remember whether they should be obeying orders preceded by nothing or by the phrase "Simon Says". The aim of this competition is not to see who wins, but to see how many rounds each individual child can last for. This can be compared to the number of rounds they lasted for in previous sessions.

Session Twelve

Game One: Start this session with the game that was offered, but not chosen, at the start of session eleven.

Game Two: Follow The Leader Two – This is an extension of the same game first played in session seven, and you will add two new commands to it. These are: 1. Flat: This action involves lying flat on the ground and before standing up again; 2. Toes: This action involves bending over and touching their toes before standing up again. The game is played as before, but this time lengthen the maximum number of commands in the list to eight (it is likely that very few of your students will manage to successfully retain a list of eight commands and then be able to do them in the required order, but it is worth pushing them to see how many they can do). **Note:** If your students find a list of eight commands too easy to follow, you can increase the number until you reach the point where they find it challenging to follow.

Game Three: Toes-Nose-Switch – This is a new game. Your students start by standing in front of you with their arms out to their sides and parallel to the floor. Start by saying "Toes" as you bend over and touch your toes (or get as close to doing it as possible). Your students need to do the same before returning to their original position. Next, say "Nose" as you bend your arms and touch the tip of your nose with both hands. Again, your students need to do the same before returning to their original position. You can then call out random commands of "Nose" and "Toes" while dong the appropriate actions, which your students need to follow. Whenever the "Switch" command is given, you need to keep doing the original actions associated with each command, but your students need to change which action they do. This means they need to not only listen to the command, but resist simply following what you are doing and instead think for themselves as to what the appropriate response is. This makes this game more challenging than if they were simply following verbal commands or actions. After five minutes of playing it, introduce a competitive element. As before, remind your students that they are not playing against each other, but that each of them has their own targets and is trying to do better than they have done in earlier sessions. As always, this session is scored based on the number of rounds that each child survives before being eliminated and this can be recorded and compared to the number of rounds they lasted for in previous sessions. You should aim to reach a point in this assessment part of the session where the instructions are too complicated for any child to successfully follow. This can be done by increasing the frequency of switch commands issued, including giving more than one switch command in a row, and by increasing the speed at which the commands of "Nose" and "Toes" are given and demonstrated.

Week Seven

Session Thirteen

Game One: For this game, provide your students with a list of three games they have played previously and ask them to vote on which game they would like to play. This increases their feeling of control and will increase their engagement.

Game Two: By this point, your students should be familiar with the basics of the games like Toes-Nose-Switch, where you select two actions and switch between them. So, for the second game in this session, ask your students to design their own game based on these principles by selecting two simple physical actions they wish to do. Then they need to decide on what commands will be used for each action, and finally they need to come up with a name for their game. Once they have done this, they are ready to start the game.

Game Three: Base Camp Three – For this game, you will need three different colours of mats, hula hoops or circles cut out to paper to function as bases. The total number of bases (regardless of their colour) should be equal to the number of children in the group. Each colour is associated with a different action. For example, a red base might be associated with jumping up and down, a blue base with spinning round and a green base with doing a Viking clap. Tell your students which action is associated with which colour. When you say "Go" they are to start running around, and when you call out "Base Camp" they need to find a base and do the action corresponding to the colour of that base. After a few seconds, call out "Go", and they can start running around again. This is then repeated. After five minutes, a competitive element is introduced, where anyone who does the wrong action on the wrong colour is eliminated. The aim of this competition is not to see who wins, but to see how many rounds each individual child can last for. This can be added to their personal self-control development sheet and compared to the number of rounds they lasted in previous sessions.

Session Fourteen

Game One: Start this session by playing the game that the children designed for themselves in session thirteen.

Game Two: Left-Right-Switch – This game not only helps with developing listening and self-control, but also right-left discrimination. Start with your students standing in front of you with their arms by their sides. Whenever you call out the name of a body part, they much touch it. For example, if you call out "Left Arm", they would need to touch their left arm, while if you call out "Right Toes", they would need to touch their right toes. Repeat this several times, but then introduce the "Switch" command. Now when you call out "Left Arm", they would need to touch their right arm instead. Repeat this for ten minutes while you use the switch command to regularly switch between the different versions of the game.

Game Three: Simon Says Switch – Again, this is the same game first played in session three. After five minutes, a competitive element is introduced, where any child who obeys a command when they shouldn't, or doesn't obey a command when they should, is eliminated. As the game progresses, you should increase the frequency of the switch command to make it more difficult for your students to remember whether they should be obeying orders preceded by nothing or by the phrase "Simon Says". The aim of this competition is not to see who wins, but to see how many rounds each individual child can last for. This can be compared to the number of rounds they lasted for in previous sessions. As always with the assessment parts of these sessions, increase the complexity of the game until none of your students are capable of successfully following them.

Week Eight

Session Fifteen

Game One: For this game, provide your students with a list three games they have played previously and ask them to vote on which game they would like to play. This increases their feeling of control and will increase their engagement.

Game Two: Mirror Image – In this game, your students form two lines facing each other, with enough space between them so that they won't accidentally hit each other. At the start, the children on the left hand side take the lead. Each one has to select one of the six actions from *Follow The Leader Two* and the child opposite them has to do the same action as quickly as possible. This encourages your students to focus on a single person and not everything else that is going on around them. When you call out "Switch", the child on the right hand side takes the lead, and the other child has to now copy their actions.

Game Three: For this session, ask your students which of the games they have played previously they would like to play to assess their self-control and listening abilities, and use this game to run the assessment following the instructions provided above.

Session Sixteen

Game One: Animal Antics – For this game, ask your students to select two types of animal they would like to behave like. When you call out the animal's name, they must behave like that animal. Use the "Switch" command to alternate between acting like the animal named, or acting like the other one.

Game Two: Four Corners – For this game, designate individual walls of the room you are playing it in as North, South, East and West. To start, your students stretch their arms out in front of them, hands clasped, and point at the wall designated North. When you call out a new direction, they must swivel round to point at that wall. When you call out "Switch" East becomes West and North becomes South. This is a higher level of complexity of remembering which action needs to be done in response to each command given.

Game Three: Follow The Leader Two – This is the same game first played in session thirteen. However, after five minutes of playing it, introduce a competitive element. As always, remind your students that they are not playing against each other, but that each of them has their own targets and is trying to do better than they have done in earlier sessions. This session is scored based on the number of rounds that each child survives before being eliminated and this can be recorded and compared to the number of rounds they lasted for in previous sessions.

This is the end of the formal programme for developing self-control in primary-aged children. At this stage, you can review each child's personal self-control development sheet with them, and hopefully they will all have shown some improvement over time. If they have, encourage them to keep trying to work on and improve this ability. Even if they haven't, make sure that they understand that self-control is not a fixed characteristic that they can do nothing about, that different children develop self-control skills at different rates and that if they keep trying, they will get better at it.

It is also worth considering regularly adding these types of games into your teaching/PE sessions with your class. This will help act as a refresher and top up your students self-control skills. In particular, it is worth using these games to help your students shift back into using good self-control skills after any holidays or breaks in their regular school routine where they may have got out of the habit of using them.

---- *Chapter Six* ----
How To Encourage Your Students To Invent Their Own Self-Control Development Games

An important part of this self-control development programme is to give your students a feeling of control over how the programme is run. This can be done in two different ways. The first is to let them select which games they wish to play as the programme develops, and the second is to ask them to invent their own games. This will give the much greater ownership over the activities in the programme and this should encourage them to try harder at them.

In order to encourage your students to invent their own games, you first need to explain the three basic types of games and what they involve. These are: Rule-switching games; location-based rules games and list-following games. Full descriptions of each of these basic types can be found in chapter three, but in brief, rule-switching games involve two basic commands for which the meaning is switched back and forth as the game is played, location-based rules games have different actions that need to be carried out tied to different spatial locations and list-following games require them to remember and follow a list of commands.

Start by asking your students to decide if they wish to invent a rule-switching game, a location-based rules game or a list-following game. Once this has been decided, ask them to select the actions that will be involved and what the associated commands will be. These actions can be things like acting like a particular type of animal, moving in particular way, or repeating a specific action (like jumping up and down or doing a star jump). Once these have been decided upon, ask them to come up with a name for their game. Finally, you need to test the game. Try it for a few rounds and then ask the children to review whether it is working as they thought it would or whether any of the rules need changing to improve it or fix any issues that have arisen with it.

Once the game has been finalised, either write out an official description of the game, including its name and how to play it, or ask your students to write it out. At this stage, you can add it into the roster of games that you will play as part of the self-control development programme. You can also task your students with teaching their game to another class in your school. This will help them learn about how to explain rules and tasks to others so that they understand what they need to do. Finally, you can also give your students copies of the official descriptions for any games they invent so that they can play them a home.

---- *Chapter Seven* ----
How To Help Your Students Track Their Self-Control Skills Development

At the end of each session in this self-control development programme there is an assessment section. This assessment section is an elimination game that your students play to see how many rounds they can survive. This provides a measure of how good their self-control skills are, and by looking at how this changes throughout the programme they can track how their self-control skills are developing. Before each of these assessments, make sure that you emphasise that the aim for each student is not necessarily to beat their classmates, but to survive for more rounds than they did on previous assessments. This ensures that those students who start with poorer self-control skills do not become discouraged from trying to improve them. To help each student monitor how well they are doing, you can provide them with a copy of the assessment sheets that you will find on the next two pages. These can be filled in at the end of each assessment so that they can see how they are doing. If any students are not improving, week-on-week, make sure that you re-assure them that this is okay, and that the important thing is that they try their hardest to improve the number of rounds they survive the next time round. In addition, it is beneficial to remind each student before the assessment what their previous highest score was and emphasise that they should try as hard as possible to beat this previous higher score. This will give them a target to work towards.

It is also worth asking your students on a regular basis to think about whether they have been using self-control skills in their daily lives, and whether there have been situations which they have found themselves in where they would have benefitted from using self-control, but where they failed to do so. This can be done by asking them to review their past week to see if they can provide examples of occasions when they successfully managed to control their cheeky chimp, occasions when it was okay to let their cheeky chimp out to play, and occasions when their cheeky chimp got them into trouble, and where they would have benefitted from trying harder to keep it under control. Once your students realise that they will need to do this on a regular basis, they will start looking for examples of these from their every day lives and this will encourage them to actively think about using self-control in their daily lives. To help with this, a handout is provided at the end of this chapter which you can ask your students to complete on a regular basis throughout this programme (and, indeed, through out the school year).

How Are My Self-Control Skills Developing?

My name is _____   My cheeky chimp's name is _____

Fill in how many rounds you successfully completed in each session, but remember, don't worry if sometimes you don't do as well as you did the time before. You can always try harder next time.

	Session 1	Session 2	Session 3	Session 4	Session 5	Session 6	Session 7	Session 8
Round 10								
Round 9								
Round 8								
Round 7								
Round 6								
Round 5								
Round 4								
Round 3								
Round 2								
Round 1								

How Are My Self-Control Skills Developing?

My name is _____ My cheeky chimp's name is _____

Fill in how many rounds you successfully completed in each session, but remember, don't worry if sometimes you don't do as well as you did the time before. You can always try harder next time.

	Session 9	Session 10	Session 11	Session 12	Session 13	Session 14	Session 15	Session 16
Round 10								
Round 9								
Round 8								
Round 7								
Round 6								
Round 5								
Round 4								
Round 3								
Round 2								
Round 1								

How Have I Used My Self-Control Skills In The Last Week?

My name is _____   My cheeky chimp's name is _____

I successfully used my self-control skills to keep my cheeky chimp from getting me into trouble when:

_____
_____
_____
_____
_____

It was okay for me to let my cheeky chimp out to play when:

_____
_____
_____
_____
_____

I lost control of my cheeky chimp when:

_____
_____
_____
_____

But I can always try harder to keep it under control next time!

---- Chapter Eight ----
Integrating Self-Control Development Into The Rest Of Your Teaching

While this self-control programme has been designed to act as a stand-alone programme, it is more likely to achieve better results if self-control development is integrated into the rest of your teaching. This will help your students see that self-control is not just an isolated skill, but it something that can be applied to many different areas of their lives, including their wider academic careers.

Using Mantras To Help Reinforce Self-Control Development

One of the best ways to reinforce the learning of life skills, including self-control, is through the use of mantras. In this context, mantras are short, easy-to-remember phrases (preferably that either rhyme or use alliteration) which can be used as a quick reminder of underlying life lessons and skills training. In the context of self-control development, this includes reminding your students to think about their actions and responses, and consider whether they are letting their cheeky chimp take over their behaviour and thought processes at times when this is not appropriate. To introduce self-control mantras into your classroom, start by using a few examples and get your students to design posters to illustrate them. Once finished, these can be put up around your classroom to act as reminders to your students.

A good starting mantra is:

> "Don't let your cheeky chimp get you into trouble."

This is a great reminder to your students that losing control of the cheeky chimp part of their brain can cause them problems. It is also a great way to warn either an individual or a whole group that their behaviour is getting out of hand and that they need to regain control of their cheeky chimps before they get into trouble.

On a similar vein, you can use:

> "Is your cheeky chimp showing?"

This encourages your students to think about whether they are acting rationally or whether they are letting their cheeky chimp take over their decision-making.

You can also use:

> "No cheeky chimps allowed in the classroom."

This reinforces the idea that while it is okay to let their cheeky chimps out to play in the playground, when they return to the classroom, they need to use their self-control skills to keep focussed and to think before they act. This is a good mantra to ask your students to illustrate and then post their artwork on your classroom door so that they see it each and every time they enter it.

Finally, you can use:

> "Always think before you do."

Again this acts as a reminder that they are expected to think rationally before they act or react, rather than simply letting their cheeky chimps respond instinctively and this requires them to apply their self-control skills.

Once your students get the hang of using these mantras, you can ask them to come up with their own, and then design a poster to go along with it. However, when doing this, is it important to make sure that any mantras they come up with are positive and encouraging in nature rather than negative.

Creating Posters To Help Identify Situations Where Self-Control Is Needed

As well as creating posters based around mantras, you can create posters to help your students identify situations where self-control is needed and when it is okay to let their cheeky chimps out to play. The best way to do this is to draw two circles on a large piece of paper. Above one of them write *No Chimps Allowed* while above the other write *Chimp's Playtime*. Next, come up with a range of different places, times, activities and situations, and write these on individual pieces of card. Turn these cards face down and ask a student to select one at random. You can then read out what it says on the selected card and ask your students to decide whether it should be placed in the *No Chimps Allowed* circle or the *Chimp's Playtime* circle. This will help your students to get into the habit of thinking whether or not they need to apply self-control in different situations they may encounter in their daily lives.

Integrating Self-Control Assessment Into Class Discipline

There will be times when poor self-control results in behaviours in your classroom that require you to take disciplinary action. In fact, when you think about it, most, if not all, such situations probably have their roots in poor self-control. As a result, it can be useful to introduce self-control assessment into classroom discipline. There are two ways to do this.

The first is to try to head off problems before they get to the point where you need to intervene. The easiest way to do this is to flag up times when a student or a group of students are starting to lose self-control and remind them that they need to re-establish it or they will get into trouble. This can be done very effectively using mantras such as "Is your cheeky chimp showing?" or "Don't let your cheeky chimp get you into trouble".

The second option is to include a discussion about self-control into any disciplinary action. In particular, you can ask a student to assess why they think they got into trouble and, in particular, whether it was their logical self or whether it was their inner cheeky chimp that caused it to happen. If they agree that they got into trouble because their cheeky chimp took over control of their thinking and their behaviour, then ask them what they think they could do if they are faced with a similar situation in the future to help keep their cheeky chimp under control. This is not to say that this should replace any punishments that you choose to impose, but rather that by adding in this type of discussion about self-control into it, it will hopefully help your students understand, and learn to identify, when they need to use self-control and, by doing this, reduce the likelihood that it will happen again.

Positive Praise And Highlighting

It is remarkable how effective positive praise can be for encouraging children to repeat desired behaviours until they become second nature to them, and developing self-control is no different. This makes it important that you positively praise your students when you see them using their self-control skills in the classroom or elsewhere in the school. Of particular benefit here is when you highlight good self-control behaviour when you see it happening spontaneously. This lets the student know both that they have been seen, and that you appreciate the effort they put in to using self-control. When doing this, make sure that you clearly spell out exactly what you saw and why you are praising them for it. This ensures that they understand what they did well, and so feel encouraged to do it again in the future. You can find more information about how best to give positive praise at *howtoraiseahappygenius.com/parental-skill-seven-ways-to-positively-praise-your-child/*.

When highlighting instances of good self-control behaviour, it is often useful to introduce *You've Been Seen* cards specific to using self-control behaviours. Depending on how you operate within your particular school, these can be traded for rewards, exchanged for ranking points or simply operate as their own rewards on charts showing who has been seen displaying good self-control behaviours.

Self-Control-based Classroom Discussions

Classroom discussions are an incredibly useful and effective way of raising awareness about self-control and helping children understand the types of situations where they need to learn to apply self-control, and the types of situations where it is okay to let their inner chimps out to play. Classroom discussions can also help children learn from each other and understand that different people can perceive the same situation in different ways. This is a particularly important life lesson for children to learn as they need to understand that they are in charge of their own decision-making and that they need to make their own judgements about whether they need to exhibit good self-control in a particular situation rather than simply relying on cues from those around them.

Classroom discussions about self-control can be based on examples from the children's own lives, from incidents in sporting events or the actions of characters in books they are reading, television programmes they watch or movies they see. However, it can be useful to divide any discussion into three basic categories: Classroom situations, social situations and life situations. Classroom situations can include things like making a mistake in class, getting into trouble for laughing at someone else's bad behaviour, not being picked to answer a question, grabbing items from another child and responding aggressively when someone else pushes into line in front of them. Social situations can include things like when another child won't let them join a game that is being played, when they are asked by a parent to do one thing when they'd rather be doing something else, when a younger child takes something from them and when someone encourages them to do something they know is wrong. Life situations can include things like wanting to get a new toy when they don't have the money to pay for it, how they respond when a favourite toy breaks, what to do if they forget to do their homework, and how to respond if they accidentally break something belonging to someone else's.

Worksheets are provided on the next three pages, one for each of these types of situation, which you can use to help stimulate classroom discussions. These present different scenarios that can be discussed, and then the children can fill in an example of how their cheeky chimp might want to respond, and an example of a better way their rational human side could respond which involves using self-control to keep their cheeky chimp in line. There is also space for the children to come up with their own scenarios which they can add these responses to as well.

Using Self-Control In Classroom Situations

My name is _____

My cheeky chimp's name is _____

Situation One

I see someone else acting silly in class

🐒 My cheeky chimp's response: _____

A better response that uses self-control: _____

Situation Two

Someone pushes in front of me in the line to go outside to play

🐒 My cheeky chimp's response: _____

A better response that uses self-control: _____

Situation Three

🐒 My cheeky chimp's response: _____

A better response that uses self-control: _____

Using Self-Control In Social Situations

My name is _____   My cheeky chimp's name is _____

Situation One

Someone won't let me join in the game they are playing

🐵 My cheeky chimp's response: _____   A better response that uses self-control: _____

Situation Two

Someone tells me they won't be my friend any more if I don't let them play with me

🐵 My cheeky chimp's response: _____   A better response that uses self-control: _____

Situation Three

_____

🐵 My cheeky chimp's response: _____   A better response that uses self-control: _____

Using Self-Control In Life Situations

My name is _____
My cheeky chimp's name is _____

Situation One

I see a new toy that I really want, but I don't have the money to pay for it.

My cheeky chimp's response: _____

A better response that uses self-control: _____

Situation Two

I accidently break something when playing at a friend's house

My cheeky chimp's response: _____

A better response that uses self-control: _____

Situation Three

My cheeky chimp's response: _____

A better response that uses self-control: _____

Word, Number, Observation And Memory Games To Help Develop Self-Control

As well as the physical games outlined in the main programme itself, there are many other types of games that you can play with your class that will not only help develop their self-control skills through enhancing their working memory, but will also develop their literacy, numeracy and observation skills.

The President's Cat

The best word games for improving working memory are those that require your students to remember lists of items. One which is often very popular is called *The President's Cat*. This is also a great game for helping to improve their use of descriptive words as it requires them to come up with words to describe a cat. This game is best played in small groups. The first child starts by saying "The President's cat is a … cat", where they fill in the blank space with a descriptive word for the cat starting with the letter A, like Angry. The next child then repeats the same description, but adds a new descriptive word beginning with the letter B (such as "The President's cat is an Angry, Bald cat", and so on. This continues until a child either fails to come up with a descriptive word starting with the appropriate letter, or fails to accurately recite the full list of previously-used descriptive words.

The Word List Game

The challenge for this game is to remember a list of words, and it is great for expanding your students' vocabulary as well as their working memories. The game itself is very simple: you provide them with a list of words that they need to remember and then recall later. They score one point for each word on the list they manage to remember. Start by selecting a list of words appropriate for your students' stage of vocabulary development and read this list out to them. Initially, start with a relatively short list. Once you have finished reading out the list ask them to write down as many of the words they can remember. This requires that they move the words between their auditory working memory and their visual/motor working memory, which makes this task more mentally strenuous than if they just had to repeat them back to you, or pick them out of a list. As your students become more proficient with this game you can lengthen the list of words they need to remember. In addition, you can also make this game more challenging by asking them to answer age-appropriate maths questions between giving them the list and having them write it down. Similarly, you can lengthen the time they have to remember them. For example, you could read them the list of words just before they go out for their morning break, and then you could ask them to recall them when they return to the classroom afterwards. If your students become really skilled at this game, try giving them the list of words at the start of the day, and seeing how many they can recall at the end of the day (or even the following morning).

The Maths Memory Game

The best number games to improve working memory are those that require a child to remember one piece of information while answering maths questions. This is because they have to continually work to recall the first bit of information while not losing track of the maths calculations they have to do. This can be integrated into learning about addition, subtraction, multiplication, division or times tables. In order to play this type of game, you first need a set of similar target objects which your students will need to remember. The easiest thing to use for this is a series of shapes of different colours. Start by showing them a set of different shapes and asking them to memorise their characteristics. For younger children, ask them to remember the shapes and colours of all the objects in the set (e.g. green triangles, blue squares, red circles), while for older children, ask then to remember the shapes, their colours, how many there are and the order they are in, and the number of them (e.g. three green triangles, two blue squares and one red circle). You then hide the target object from them. Next, ask them a mathematical question appropriate to their stage of development (like what is three add one or five times six). Once they have worked out the answer to this question, ask them to recall the characteristics of the shapes you asked them to remember. If they succeed, repeated this process with a new set of target objects, but this time you ask them to answer two mathematical questions before telling you what the target objects were. You can then carry on increasing the number and complexity of the mathematical questions, and the speed they need to answer them at, until they fail to recall the target object you asked them to remember.

The Observation Game

This game is similar to the word list game, but it uses a set of objects all shown at once, rather than a list of words read in sequence. For this game, gather a wide range of different, but easy-to-identify, everyday objects that you can put on a single tray and take a photograph of it. The items you put on the tray can be things like scissors, a watch, a battery, a spoon, a small toy, and so on. The aim of this game is for your students to remember as many of the different objects as possible. To start this game, tell your students that you are going to show them a picture with a number of different everyday objects in it, and they need to see how many of them they can remember. Now, show them the photograph of the tray of items for thirty seconds before hiding it again. Once it is hidden, ask the children to write down as many of the objects as they can remember. As they get better at this game, you can increase the number of objects, shorten the length of time they have to memorise the objects, and/or lengthen the time they have to remember them. For example, you could show them the objects just before they go out for their morning break, and then you could ask them to recall them when they return to the classroom afterwards. If your students become really skilled at this game, try showing them the objects at the start of the day, and seeing how many they can recall at the end of the day, or even the following morning.

The Stroop Effect Game

This is a simple, fun, but challenging game to play. Before you start this game, create a PowerPoint slide show featuring the names of different colours with some written in the same colour as their meaning (e.g. then word Red written in red), but others written in different colours (e.g. the word Red written in blue). To play this game, simply show your students these slides one by one and ask them to call out the colour each one is written in, rather than the meaning of the word itself. This is surprisingly complicated and it requires them to resist calling out the wrong answer. As they get better at this, you can shorten the time that each word is shown for. In addition, just like the physical games played in the main programme, you can make this game more strenuous for their working memories by introducing a "Switch" command, meaning they have to switch between calling out the colour the word is written in, and the meaning of the word itself. This game is named after the Stroop Effect, which is the fact that our brains find it harder to read a word, and are more prone to making errors, when the colour it is written in conflicts with its meaning. Interestingly, students with dyslexia may be much better at calling out the colour that the word is written in when it doesn't match its meaning because they are not distracted by the meaning of the word itself. This can be a nice demonstration of how people with conditions such as dyslexia can actually perform better than other people at certain tasks because of the different way their brains work.

Reminding Your Students When The Use Of Self-Control Is Appropriate And When It Is Acceptable To Let Their Cheeky Chimps Out To Play

Many children will, quite naturally, exhibit a bleed of poor self-control when they move from a situation where it is acceptable to let their cheeky chimps out to play to a situation where it is not. For example, you will frequently see a bleed of poor self-control behaviour between playtime or lunchtime and the return to the classroom. This is because it requires practice to identify when a situation has changed and then to successfully reign in their cheeky chimps and bring them back under control when they have previously been let out to play. You can help your students learn to identify when such switches in what is considered acceptable behaviour occur, and to respond accordingly, by using simple, non-judgemental reminders to highlight when they are moving from situations where it is acceptable to let their inner cheeky chimps out to play to ones where it is not. If you can integrate these into your usual classroom routine, it should not only minimise disruption caused by inappropriate chimp-driven behaviour, it should also encourage and help your students to learn to identify when they move from one type of situation to another and to alter their behaviour accordingly.

A useful pair of reminders that you can use to verbally label these different types of situations are "Let your chimps run free!" when they switch to a situation where some (but not all) chimp-driven behaviours are acceptable (like during playtime) and "Chimps Away!" when they switch to a situation where they need to bring their inner cheeky chimps back under control (like when then return to the classroom after their break). Once these labels have been established in your students minds, you will find that you can use them in a wide range of situations, including during activities such as school trips, to help them regulate their own behaviour, and hopefully make your life easier.

You can also help your students understand these types of switches in acceptable behaviour by playing a game of *Chimp Away, Chimp Play*. This is a simple game where you give them a situation and ask them to decide whether it is acceptable to let their inner chimps out to play (which they can indicate by moving to an area of your classroom that you have designated for the answer "Chimp Play") or whether it is not (which they can indicate by moving to an area of your classroom that you have designated for the answer "Chimp Away"). Once they have all moved to the appropriate area, tell them that the situation has changed and describe the new situation to them before asking if they now need to change how they are dealing with their cheeky chimp (which they can indicate by moving to area designated for the opposite answer) or not (which they can indicate by remaining where they currently are). For example, you might start with a initial situation of playing in the park after school (when it would be acceptable to let their cheeky chimp out to play) and then ask them what would be appropriate if they then have to go shopping with their parents, and whether they need to change how they have been dealing with their cheeky chimp to adapt to the new situation they find themselves in. Similarly, you could take them through a typical school day, starting with playing in the playground with their friends before morning bell rings and ask them to identify when there are changes between when it is okay to let their cheeky chimps out to play, and when it is not. Finally, if you are planning a school trip, you can prime your students about when it will be okay for them to let their chimps out to play during the trip, and when they will need to bring their cheeky chimps under control by taking them through the situations they will encounter in advance of doing the trip itself. This can be done the day before, before departing the school, or while travelling to the location of the trip.

---- Chapter Nine ----
Additional Reading On Self-Control And Its Importance For Child Development

If you wish to read more about self-control, and its importance for child development, you can check out the following resources:

1. *The Marshmallow Test*: This book by Walter Mischel is probably the best source of information on self-control, delayed gratification, and the important roles they play in creating children who grow into happy and successful adults.

2. *The Chimp Paradox: The Mind Management Programme For Confidence, Success And Happiness*: This book by Steve Peters provides an outline of the chimp mind management programme on which many aspects of the self-control development programme presented in this book are based.

3. *The Silent Guides: Understanding And Developing The Mind Throughout Life*: This book by Steve Peters provides advice and information for adults on how they can help develop the minds of children and young adults using the mind management programme presented in *The Chimp Paradox*.

4. *My Hidden Chimp*: This book by Steve Peters aims to help children and young adults understand and use the mind management programme presented in *The Chimp Paradox*.

5. **Teaching Self-Control: Evidence-Based Tips:** This is a great article from *ParentingScience.com* about self-control and how to encourage its development in your child. You can find it at *www.parentingscience.com/teaching-self-control.html*.

6. **The Marshmallow Test And Why We Want Instant Gratification:** This TedEx talk from YouTube will also help you understand why delayed gratification is important. You can find it at *youtu.be/voF8B-Jr0mA*.

7. **Forget Delayed Gratification, What Children Really Need Is Cognitive Control:** Despite what the title of this article implies, it isn't really anti-delayed gratification. Instead, it is emphasising that delayed gratification, while important, isn't the be-all-and-end-all that some people might claim. You can read this article at *ideas.time.com/2013/10/07/forget-delayed-gratification-what-kids-really-need-is-cognitive-control/*.

www.ingramcontent.com/pod-product-compliance
Lightning Source LLC
Chambersburg PA
CBHW050715090526
44587CB00019B/3395